Let Go Of Whatever Makes You Stop

by

John L. Mason

Sixteenth printing

Over 175,000 in print

Let Go of Whatever Makes You Stop
ISBN 0-88419-373-X
Copyright © 1994 by John Mason
Published by Insight International
P.O. Box 54996
Tulsa, Oklahoma 74155
www.freshword.com

Contents

DEDICATION

To Dave, for his joy that reminds me to
have a smile on my face;

to Mike, for his energy and inquisitiveness
that reminds me to be creative;

to Greg, for his patience that reminds me
to take small steps;

to Michelle, for her love of music that reminds me
to live a life of praise;

and to my wife, Linda, for her commitment to God that
reminds me to be a man of right priorities.

ACKNOWLEDGMENTS

To three great friends:

Mike Loomis, thanks for your humor and agreement;

Tim Redmond, thanks for your prophetic insight
into my life;

Tom Winters, thanks for helping me to "take the lid off"
my thinking.

Also, a special thanks to Leyna Blackbird-Irby for her
cheerful help in typing this book;

and to Deborah Poulalion for her challenging and
excellent editing.

INTRODUCTION

Momentum—what a great word for a powerful life. I believe without a doubt that God's will for you is momentum. He wants you to let go of whatever makes you stop—to grow, to increase, to be more than what you are today.

These are the characteristics of momentum: 1) It is single-minded; 2) it is unwavering in the pursuit of a goal; 3) it has passion which knows no limits; 4) it demands a concentrated intensity and a definite sense of destiny; and, most of all, 5) it has a boundless vision and commitment to excellence.

As a result of reading this book, I believe you will capture and increase momentum in your life. The Bible says you can be "confident of this very thing, that he which hath begun a good work in you will perform it until the day of Jesus Christ" (Phil. 1:6).

Be confident and receive God's momentum for your life.

LOOKING
INWARD

NUGGET # 1

A Diamond Is A Hunk Of Coal That Stuck To Its Job And Made Good Under Pressure.

Our daily prayer should be, "Lord, give me the determination and tenacity of a weed." It's been said that a great oak is only a little nut that held its ground. "These troubles and sufferings of ours are, after all, quite small and won't last very long. Yet this short time of distress will result in God's richest blessing upon us forever and ever!" (2 Cor. 4:17, TLB). Many of us take hold of opportunity, but we let go of it too soon.

Don B. Owens, Jr. said it so well: "Many people fail in life because they believe in the adage: 'If you don't succeed, try something else.' But success eludes those who follow such advice. The dreams that came true did so because people stuck to their ambitions. They refused to be discouraged. They never let disappointment get the upper hand. Challenges only spurred them on to greater efforts." You will be judged by what you finish, not by what you start. If you don't see results right away, don't worry. God does not pay by the week, but He pays at the end.

All great achievements require time and tenacity. Be persevering because the last key on the ring may be the one that opens the door. Hanging on one second longer than your competition makes you a winner. Become famous for finishing important, difficult tasks.

If you are ever tempted to stop, just think of Brahms, who took seven long years to compose his famous lullaby because he kept falling asleep at the piano – just kidding, but it did take him seven years to finish. I agree with Woodrow Wilson when he said, "I would rather fail in a cause that will ultimately succeed than succeed in a cause that will ultimately fail." Ninety percent of all failures result from people quitting too soon. "And let us not get tired of doing what is right, for after a while we will reap a harvest of blessing if we don't get discouraged and give up" (Gal. 6:9, TLB). It takes the hammer of persistence to drive the nail of success.

Many people who fail did not realize how close they were to success when they gave up. Harriet Beecher Stowe wrote: "When you get into a tight place and everything goes against you until it seems as though you could not hold on a minute longer, never give up then, for that is just the time and place that the tide will turn."

You always uncover opportunity by applying persistence to possibilities. When you get right down to the root meaning of the word *succeed*, you find that it simply means "to persevere and follow through." Any diamond will tell you that it was just a hunk of coal that stuck to its job and made good under pressure.

The road to success runs uphill, so don't expect to break any speed records. Impatience is costly. Your greatest mistakes will happen because of impatience. Most people fail simply because they're impatient and they cannot join the beginning with the end.

"The determined soul will do more with a rusty monkey wrench than a loafer will accomplish with all the tools in a mechanic's shop," says Rupert Hughs. The power to hold on in spite of everything, to endure—this is the winners quality.

NUGGET #2

When You're Trying To Be Like Someone Else, The Best You Can Ever Be Is Number Two.

You and I are born equal but also different. Do you want to stand out in the world? Then be yourself. Be what you really are. This is the first step toward becoming better than what you are now. "No man could be ideally successful until he has found his place. Like a locomotive, he is strong on the track, but weak anywhere else" (Orsen Marden). Choose to become yourself.

Avoid following the crowd. Be an engine, not a caboose. As Herman Melville wrote: "It is better to fail in originality than to succeed in imitation." Average people would rather be wrong than be different. We relinquish three-fourths of ourselves in order to be like other people. Conformity is the jailer of satisfaction and the enemy of growth. Did you know you're destined to be different? Dare to be different and follow your own star.

"Be yourself. Who else is better qualified?" (Frank Giblin). Ask yourself two questions. If I try to be like him, who will be like me? If I'm not me, who will I be? The more you develop your potential, the less you will become like someone else. Trying to be like someone else is self-defeating. One of your main purposes in life is to give birth to yourself. As long as you are trying to be like someone else, the best you can ever be is number two.

We can't reach our destiny taking another man's road. He who never walks except where he sees another man's tracks will make no new discoveries. "Do not follow where the path may lead—go instead where there is no path and leave a trail" (Unknown). "God has given each of us the ability to do certain things well" (Rom. 12:6, TLB).

"Don't let the world around you squeeze you into its own mold, but let God remake you so that your whole attitude of mind is changed" (Rom. 12:2, Phillips). "The more you are like yourself, the less you are like anyone else" (Walt Disney). You are like a tree—you must put forth the fruit that's created in you.

You can't be common. The common goes nowhere. You must be uncommon to be a champion. Your responsibility is not to remake yourself, but to make the absolute best of what God made. Don't compromise yourself...it's all you've got. "Almost every man wastes part of his life in attempts to display qualities he does not possess" (Samuel Johnson). Don't let your life be a continual struggle to be what you are not, and to do what you should not.

You are an unprecedented miracle. You are as God made you, and since He is satisfied, you should be too.

NUGGET #3

People Say They Want Riches. What They Need Is Fulfillment Of A Purpose.

The world makes room for the man of purpose. His words and actions demonstrate that he knows where he is going. You are built to conquer circumstances, solve problems and attain goals. You'll find no real satisfaction or happiness in life without obstacles to conquer, goals to achieve and a purpose to accomplish. People say they want riches; what they need is fulfillment of a purpose. Happiness comes when we squander ourselves for a purpose.

In your heart there is a sleeping lion. Be on a mission. Have a definite sense of direction and purpose for your life. Successful lives are motivated by dynamic purpose. God can only bless your plan and direct you in accomplishing it if you have one. Strong convictions precede great actions.

As soon as you resign yourself to fate, your resignation is promptly accepted. You don't have a fate; you have a purpose. When you look into the future, you'll see it's so bright it will make you squint. I'm encouraged by George Elliott, who said, "It's never too late to be what you might have been."

"More men fail through lack of purpose than lack of talent" (Billy Sunday). If your method is "hit or miss," you'll usually miss. "If you're not sure where you are going, you'll probably end up someplace else" (Robert F. Mager). Too many people don't know where they're going, but they're on their way. Growth for the sake of growth is the ideology of the cancer cell. Go forward with purpose.

Lord Chesterfield wrote: "Firmness of purpose is one of the most necessary sinews of character and one of the best instruments of success. Without it, genius wastes its efforts in a maze of inconsistencies." You are sure to find another cross if you flee the one you are to carry. The man who has no direction is the slave of his circumstances. The poorest man is not he who is without a cent, but he who is without purpose. "The only thing some people do is grow older" (Ed Howe).

"If you don't have a vision for your life, then you probably haven't focused in on anything" (Dr. David Burns). In the absence of vision there can be no clear and constant focus. Once your purpose is clear, decisions will jump at you. "When you discover your mission, you will feel its demand. It will fill you with enthusiasm and a burning desire to get to work on it" (W. Clement Stone).

NUGGET #4

Don't Live Within
Your Means.

It doesn't happen often, but while I was writing this book I was awakened in the middle of the night by the Lord. I felt Him leading me to write a nugget titled, "Don't live within your means." Even though it was 4:50 a.m., I was so excited about this that I awoke my wife and began to "preach" to her about it for several minutes. (She said the idea was great, but she really needed her sleep).

What do I believe God means when He says, "Don't live within your means?" I believe He wants us to act bigger, to believe larger, to associate higher, to (with God) do more than we can ask or think. Your outlook determines your outcome. If God is your partner...make your plans BIG.

I'm not encouraging you to go wild, to have no boundaries or to be reckless. Certainly we should spend within our means–but not live there. Talk with people smarter than you. Listen to those more spiritual than you. Ask questions of those more successful than you. Lend a hand to those less fortunate than you. Don't stay where you are.

I sincerely believe that many people who think they are frugal aren't really frugal. Rather, they are full of fear. The label of frugality, balance or conservativeness is often a mask to cover up a deep-rooted fear in their lives. Don't make such thorough plans for rainy days that you don't enjoy today's sunshine.

When you only live within your means, you can't live by faith. If you aren't living by faith, you can't please God for "without faith it is impossible to please him" (Heb. 11:6). Abandon altogether the search for security. "Only the insecure strive for security" (Wayne Dyer). If you're just trying to earn a living, you'll forget how to live.

Keith Provance, a man who has greatly influenced my life, said something I've never forgotten. He said, "Who God calls, He equips. Who He equips, He anoints to do the job." No matter what the level of your ability, God has equipped you and anointed you with more potential than you can use in your lifetime. Don't let the future be that time when you wish you'd done what you aren't doing now.

If the shoe fits, don't wear it. If you do, you're not allowing for growth. Webster knew all about the ineffectiveness of "living within your means." When you look up the word "means" in his dictionary, it tells you to see the word "average." An average life is the result of living within your means.

NUGGET #5

If You're Not Failing, You're Not Growing.

The greatest mistake you can make in life is to be continually fearing you will make one. "Don't be afraid to fail. Don't waste energy trying to cover up failure. If you're not failing, you're not growing," says H. Stanley Judd. When successful people stop growing and learning it is because they become less and less willing to risk failure. "Failure is delay, not defeat. It is a temporary detour, not a dead-end street" (William A. Ward).

We all make mistakes—especially those who do things. Failure is often the first necessary step toward success. If we don't take the risk of failing, we won't get the chance to succeed. When we are trying, we are winning. To fail is the natural consequence of trying. "Never let the fear of striking out get in your way" (Babe Ruth, strike out king, home run king).

Stop trying to be perfect. When you have a serious decision to make, tell yourself firmly you are going to make it. Do not expect that it will be a perfect one. I love the wisdom of Winston Churchill: "The maxim, 'Nothing avails but perfection,' may be spelled paralysis." Henry Ward Beecher wrote: "I don't like these cold, precise, perfect people who, in order not to speak wrong, never speak at all, and in order not to do wrong, never do anything." The pursuit of excellence is gratifying and healthy; the pursuit of perfection is frustrating, unproductive and a terrible waste of time.

The fact is that you're like a tea bag. You won't know your own strength until you get into some hot water. Failure is something we can only avoid by saying nothing, doing nothing and being nothing. "Remember, there are two benefits of failure. First, if you do fail, you learn what doesn't work; and second, the failure gives you an opportunity to try a new approach" (Roger Von Oech).

Some defeats are only installments to victory. Henry Ford noted, "Even a mistake may turn out to be the one thing necessary to a worthwhile achievement." Some people learn from their mistakes; some never recover from them. Learn how to fail intelligently. Develop success from failure.

Discouragement and failure are two of the surest stepping stones to success. No other elements can do so much for a man if he is willing to study them and to make the most out of them. "Most people think of success and failure as opposites, but they are actually both products of the same process" (Roger Von Oech). Your season of failure is the best time for sowing your seeds of success. Successful people are not afraid to fail. They go from failure to failure until at last success is theirs. The best way to accelerate your success is to double your failure rate. The law of failure is one of the most powerful of all success laws.

"No matter what mistakes you have made—no matter how you've messed things up—you can still make a new beginning. The person who fully realizes this suffers less from the shock and pain of failure and sooner gets off to a new beginning," said Norman Vincent Peale.

NUGGET #6

Constantly Frustrate Tradition With Your Creativity And Imagination.

Stop and daydream once in awhile. You need to let your imagination roam and give it a chance to breathe. It's never too late for you to start thinking more creatively. Often it is just a lack of imagination that keeps a man from his potential. Thinking of new ideas is like shaving: if you don't do it every day, you're a bum. Have a constant flow of new, exciting and powerful ideas on which you act immediately.

Constantly frustrate tradition with your creativity and imagination. "The opportunities of man are limited only by his imagination. But so few have imagination that there are ten thousand fiddlers to one composer" (Charles Kettering). Your dreams are a preview to your greatness. All men who have achieved great things have been dreamers. It may be that those who do most, dream most. A shallow thinker seldom makes a deep impression. We act, or fail to act, not because of *will*, as is so commonly believed, but because of *vision*. Only when you see the invisible can you do the impossible.

"Ideas are like rabbits. You get a couple and learn how to handle them, and pretty soon you have a dozen" (Anonymous). You'll get more out of every part of your life if you stay incurably curious. "The important thing is to not stop questioning. Never lose a holy curiosity" (Albert Einstein). Dexter Yager says, "Don't let anybody steal your dream."

"We've got to have a dream if we are going to make a dream come true" (Denis Waitley). Nothing happens unless there's a dream first. The more you can dream, the more you can do. "Ideas are like the stars: we never reach them, but, like the mariners of the sea, we chart our course by them" (Carl Schurz). "Since it doesn't cost a dime to dream, you'll never short-change yourself when you stretch your imagination" (Robert Schuller). Look at things not as they are, but as they can be. Vision adds value to everything. A single idea—the sudden flash of any thought—may be worth a million dollars.

God gave us a world unfinished so we might share in the joys and satisfaction of creation. Ted Engstrom explains: "Creativity has been built into every one of us; it's part of our design. Each of us lives less of the life God intended for us when we choose not to live out the creative powers we possess."

"I'm a big fan of dreams. Unfortunately, dreams are the first casualty in life—people seem to give them up quicker than anything for a 'reality' " (Kevin Costner). "Realistic people with practical aims are rarely as realistic or practical in the long-run of life as the dreamers who pursue their dreams" (Hans Selye).

What you need is an idea. Be brave enough to live creatively.

NUGGET #7

Get Ahead During The Time Others Waste.

Don't be a person who says, "Ready! Aim, aim, aim, aim." As fast as each opportunity presents itself, use it! No matter how small the opportunity may be, use it! Do the thing you need to do when it ought to be done whether you like it or not. "He who hesitates misses the green light, gets bumped in the rear, and loses his parking space" (Herbert Prochnow).

One of the deceptions of an unproductive life is that today is not the critical, important, decisive day. Every day comes bearing its gifts. Untie the ribbons, tear into the wrapping, open it up. Write on your heart every day that it is the best day of the year.

By the time the fool has learned to play the game, the players have dispersed, and the rules have changed. Don't find yourself striking when the iron is cold. Instead, scratch opportunity where it itches. Life is made of constant calls to action.

"Successful leaders have the courage to take action while others hesitate" (John Maxwell). You never know what you can do until you try. Remember, the moment you say, "I give up," someone else is seeing the same situation and saying, "My, what a great opportunity." The fact is that no opportunity is ever lost; someone else picks up those you missed. A secret of success in life is to be ready for opportunity when it comes. Ability is nothing apart from opportunity.

Time flies. It's up to you to be the pilot. "Everything comes to him who hustles while he waits" (Thomas Edison). It has been my observation that most people get ahead during the time that others waste. A secret of success is to do something else in the meantime. Make quick use of the moment.

It is later than you think. Be ready now. God's alarm clock has no snooze button. It doesn't do any good to "stand up and take notice" if you sit down as soon as opportunity comes by. Look at it, size it up, make a decision. You postpone your life when you can't make up your mind. "If you wait for perfect conditions, you will never get anything done...Keep on sowing your seed, for you never know which will grow—perhaps it all will" (Eccl. 11:4,6, TLB).

William Ward has a recipe for success: "Study while others are sleeping; work while others are loafing; prepare while others are playing and dream while others are wishing." There is no time like the present and no present like time. Those who take advantage of their advantage get the advantage in this world. Don't find yourself at the end of your life saying, "What a wonderful life I've had! I only wish I'd realized it sooner."

NUGGET #8

Get Out Of The Middle Of The Road.

Your destiny is not a matter of chance; it is a matter of choice. Many people have the right aims in life—they just never get around to pulling the trigger. When you determine what you want, you have made the most important decision in your life. You have to know what you want in order to attain it.

"Commit your way to the Lord, trust also in Him, and He will do it" (Ps. 37:5, NAS). If we are faithful, God will look after our success. Success is the result of a deliberate decision, an adjustment of your life to the will of God. Guidance means that I can count on God. Commitment means that God can count on me.

Harvey Cox said, "Not to decide is to decide." Weeds grow easily in the soil of indecision. Get out of the middle of the road. Standing in the middle of the road is very dangerous; you can get knocked down by traffic going both directions. The train of failure usually runs on the track of indecision.

Because of indecision, one can die before one actually is dead. "Indecision is debilitating; it feeds upon itself; it is, one might say, habit forming. Not only that, but it is contagious; it transmits itself to others" (H. A. Hopf).

"There is a fine difference of perspective between getting involved and being committed. In ham and eggs, the chicken is involved, but the pig is committed" (John Alan Price). Until one is committed, there is hesitancy, the chance to draw back, and always ineffectiveness. "I will," is a slogan for an exciting life.

You must choose between boredom and decisions. Don't be like a wheelbarrow—going no further than you are pushed by others. The weak are always forced to decide between alternatives that others have set before them, not the ones they've chosen for themselves. It's true what Mike Murdock says, "Never complain about what you permit."

A wise man makes his own decisions; an ignorant man follows public opinion. You are where you are today because you've chosen to be there. Reality forms around a commitment, and one person with commitment always accomplishes more than a hundred people with just an interest. Commitment is what transforms an idea into a reality.

Be decisive even if it means you'll sometimes be wrong. The key to your future is that you can still choose. What you commit yourself to be will change you from what you are into what you can be.

NUGGET #9

What You See Depends Mainly On What You Look For.

The reason many people don't get answers from God is the same reason a thief does not find a policeman: he is running away. How we position ourselves to receive makes all the difference. To one person the world is desolate, dull and empty; to another the same world looks rich, interesting and full of meaning. The choice is up to you. It's the same way a twenty dollar bill can look so big when it goes to church and so small when it goes for groceries.

If you look at life the wrong way there is always cause for alarm. What you see depends mainly on what you look for. Most people complain because roses have thorns. Instead be thankful that thorns have roses.

Position yourself to receive, not resist. How you see things on the outside of you depends on how things are on the inside of you. "Any fact facing us is not as important as our attitude toward it, for that determines our success or failure" (Norman Vincent Peale). "You and I do not see things as they are. We see things as we are" (Herb Cohen). Develop the hunter's approach – the outlook that wherever you go, there are ideas waiting to be discovered. When you are positioned right, opportunity presents itself.

Opportunity can be missed if you are broadcasting when you should be tuning in. When opportunity knocks, some people object to the interruption. "One of the greatest and most comforting truths is that when one door opens, another closes, but often we look so long and regretfully upon the closed door that we do not see the one that is open for us" (Anonymous).

See success where others see only failure. Expect something good to happen. That expectation will energize your dreams and give them momentum. You'll often find that life responds to your outlook. We go where our vision is. Life is mostly a matter of expectation.

You'll gain the advantage by doing things before they need to be done—positioning yourself ahead of time. You'll enjoy more success when you travel a little bit in advance of the crowd. I believe one of the major benefits of reading the Bible is that it can teach us how to respond in advance to many of life's challenges and opportunities. Dig a well before you are thirsty, and plant a seed before you are hungry.

The trouble with the future for most people is that it arrives before they are ready for it. Positioning yourself to receive causes you to be ready. The most important question is: Are you ready?

NUGGET #10

When You Excuse Yourself, You Accuse Yourself.

"Ninety-nine percent of failures come from people who have a habit of making excuses" (George Washington Carver). You are never a failure until you begin to blame somebody else. Stop blaming others. You'll find that when you become good at making excuses you won't be good at anything else. Excuses are the tools a person with no purpose or vision uses to build great monuments of emptiness.

Most people would learn from their mistakes if they weren't so busy denying and defending them. "It seems to me these days that people who admit they're wrong get a lot further than people who prove they're right" (Deryl Pfizer). What poison is to food, alibis are to a productive life. "Work brings profit; talk brings poverty" (Prov. 14:23, TLB). "Some men have thousands of reasons why they cannot do what they want to do when all they really need is one reason why they can" (Willis Whitney). Find a reason why you can.

One of the biggest alibis is regret. Don't leave any regrets on the field—give your all in the game of life. "The most valuable thing I have learned from life is to regret nothing" (Somerset Maugham). Eliminate all your regrets. I believe the mass of people live lives of quiet regret. "Regret is an appalling waste of energy; you can't build on it. It's only good for wallowing in" (Catherine Mansfield). The truth is a thousand regrets do not pay one debt. Live your life so that your tombstone reads, "No regrets."

When a winner makes a mistake, he says, "I was wrong." When a loser makes a mistake, he says, "It wasn't my fault." Do you admit it and say, "I was wrong," or do you say, "It wasn't my fault?" A winner explains, a loser explains away.

Idle people lack no excuses. The word *can't* really means you won't try. The word *can't* is the worst word that has ever been written or spoken, doing more harm than slander or lies. *Can't* is the worst excuse and the best enemy of success.

We have many reasons for failure but not a single excuse. "Excuses always replace progress" (Ralph Waldo Emerson). "In everything you do, stay away from complaining and arguing, so that no one can speak a word of blame against you" (Phil. 2:14-15, TLB). Alibis and excuses should be cremated, not embalmed. Excuses are of no avail before God. He who excuses himself always accuses himself because denying a fault doubles it.

"The best years of your life are the ones in which you decide your problems are your own. You don't blame them on your mother, the ecology or the President. You realize that you control your own destiny" (Albert Ellis). We should live our lives like Florence Nightingale when she said, "I attribute my success to this: I never gave or took an excuse."

NUGGET #11

Bite Off More Than
You Can Chew.

Don't do anything that doesn't require faith. The key to momentum is always having something in faith to look forward to. We live by faith, or we don't live at all. Either we venture, or we vegetate. What is needed is more people who specialize in the impossible. This year's success was last year's impossibility. "Faith is not trying to believe something regardless of the evidence. Faith is daring to do something regardless of the consequence" (Sherwood Eddy).

Phillips Brooks says to pray this way: "Do not pray for easy lives. Pray to be stronger men. Do not pray for tasks equal to your power. Pray for power equal to your tasks." Jesus said of you and I, "I am come that they might have life, and that they might have it more abundantly" (John 10:10). Never be afraid to do what God tells you to do. "Shoot for the moon. Even if you miss it, you will land among the stars" (Les Brown). You and I are like rubber bands. We are most useful when we are stretched.

You can only accomplish in proportion to what you attempt. The reason why so little is accomplished is generally because so little is attempted. Never say never. You have to think big to be big. "It is not because things are difficult that we do not dare; it is because we do not dare that things are difficult" (Seneca). The definition of impossible: something nobody can do until somebody does. The fact is, it's fun to do the impossible. When we're playing it safe, we create the most insecurity. So, look at things...as they can be.

You do not tap the resources of God until you attempt the impossible. Risk is part of God's plan. "I can do everything God asks me to with the help of Christ who gives me the strength and power" (Phil. 4:13, TLB). "Mediocre minds usually dismiss anything which reaches beyond their own understanding" (Rochfoucauld). Even a coward can praise Christ, but it takes a man of courage to follow Him. Calvin Coolidge said, "We do not need more intellectual power, we need more spiritual power. We do not need more things that are seen, we need more of the things that are unseen."

Progress always involves risk. You can't steal second base and keep your foot on first. He who does not dare will not get his share. Unless you enter the beehive, you cannot take the honey.

Look for ways to flex your risk muscle. Everyone has a risk muscle, and you keep it in the proper shape by experimenting and trying new things. "People who take risks are the people you'll lose against" (John Scully). "The people who are really failures are the people who set their standards so low, keep the bar at such a safe level, that they never run the risk of failure" (Robert Schuller).

A great ship always asks for deep water. When you dare for nothing you should hope for nothing. God wants us to bite off more than we can chew, to live by faith and not by sight.

NUGGET #12

Questions.

Both enthusiasm and pessimism are contagious. How much of each do you spread?

If someone were to pay you ten dollars for each kind word you spoke and collect five dollars for each unkind word, would you be rich or poor?

"What progress are you standing in the way of?" (Tim Redmond)

Are you a creature of circumstance or a creator of circumstance?

Are you ready for your opportunity when it comes?

Do you make others feel bigger or smaller when they're around you?

Are you spending your life to answer questions nobody is asking?

Ten years from today, what will you wish you had done now?

If you have God's promise for something, isn't that enough?

Why worry when you can pray?

How old is your attitude?

Are you ready?

Do you acquire the doubts of others?

Are you willing to follow the truth no matter where it leads?

Do you share your hurts or memorize them?

How much has it cost you to worry about things that never happened?

Do you go *through* a problem or try to go *around* it and never get *past* it?

Do you say, "There ought to be a better way to do it," or do you say,

"That's the way it's always been done?"

Are you deliberately planning to be less than you are capable of being?

If not you, then who? If not now, then when? (Hillell)

Are you willing to give up what you have in order to become what you can be?

What do you believe in the depth of your being?

How can you get from here to wherever it is you want to be?

What is the first, small step you can take to get moving?

Are you thinking of security or opportunity?

"If you don't have a dream, how are you going to make a dream come true?" (Oscar Hammerstein)

Do you look at the horizon and see an opportunity, or do you look into the distance and fear a problem?

Do you put off until tomorrow the things you've already put off until today?

Has failure gone to your head?

Does your reach exceed your grasp?

"Do you spend the first six days of each week sewing wild oats, then go to church on Sunday and pray for a crop failure?" (Fred Allen)

Are you traveling or going somewhere?

Are you always ready to live but never living?

Do you see difficulties in every opportunity, or do you see opportunities in every difficulty?

How many people of great potential have you known? Where on earth did they all go?

Are you content with failure?

NUGGET #13

Change, But Don't Stop.

When you're through changing, you're through. Most people fail in life because they're unwilling to make changes. But the fact is that correction and change always result in fruit.

All mankind is divided into three classes: 1) those who are unchangeable; 2) those who are changeable and 3) those who cause change. "Change is always hardest for the man who is in a rut, for he has scaled down his living to that which he can handle comfortably and welcomes no change or challenge that would lift him up," wrote C. Neil Strait. If you find yourself in a hole, stop digging. When things go wrong–don't go with them. Stubbornness and unwillingness to change is the energy of fools.

"He that will not apply new remedies must expect new evils," observed Francis Bacon. "I will instruct you (says the Lord) and guide you along the best pathway for your life; I will advise you and watch your progress" (Ps. 32:8, TLB). God never closes one door without opening another one, but we must be willing to change in order to walk through that new door.

In prayer we learn to change. Prayer is one of the most changing experiences we will ever know. You cannot pray and stay the same.

Playing it safe is probably the most unsafe thing in the world. You cannot stand still. You must go forward and be open to those adjustments that God has for you. The most unhappy people are those who fear change.

It's been said many times: you can't make an omelet without breaking eggs. Accomplishment automatically results in change.

One change makes way for the next, giving us the opportunity to grow. You must change to master change.

You've got to be open to change because every time you think you're ready to graduate from the school of experience, somebody thinks up a new course. Decide to be willing to experience change. If you can figure out where to stand firm and when to bend, you've got it made. We can become nervous because of incessant change, but we would be frightened if the change were stopped.

Blessed is the man who can adjust to a set of circumstances without surrendering his convictions. Open your arms to change, but don't let go of your values. The majority of people meet with failure because of a lack of persistence in developing new ideas and plans to take place of those which failed. Your growth depends on your willingness to experience change.

NUGGET #14

It's Passion That Persuades.

The starting point of all accomplishment is desire. Keep this in mind: feeble desires bring feeble results just as a small amount of fire makes a small amount of heat. Be passionate about your life. Act from your passions. Know that the more energy you apply to any task, the more you will have to apply to the next task. "Whatsoever thy hand findeth to do, do it with thy might" (Eccl. 9:10).

Desire is the planting of your seed. It sometimes seems that deep desire creates not only its own opportunities, but its own talents. "A strong passion for any object will insure success, for the desire of the end will point out the means" (William Hazlitt).

The trouble with many educated men is that learning goes to their heads and not to their hearts. The heart is something of a prophet. The heart is no traitor. It is only with the heart that one can see correctly; what is required is invisible to the eye. Does the path you're traveling capture your heart? God has sent you into this world to do something into which you can pour your heart.

You will only be remembered in life for your passions. Find something that consumes you. A belief is not just an idea a person possesses; it is an idea that possesses a person. "Whatsoever ye do, do it heartily, as to the Lord, and not unto men" (Col 3:23). Learn to be comfortable with being enthusiastic.

Every time zeal and passion are discussed someone brings up *balance*. Balance is a tremendous virtue, but the immediate neighbors of balance are apathy and weakness. If the truth were known, being balanced is usually an excuse for being lukewarm, indifferent or neutral. Indifference, lukewarmness, and neutrality are always attached to failure.

Enthusiasm can achieve in one day what it takes centuries to achieve by reason. "Above all else, guard your affections. For they influence everything else in your life" (Prov. 4:23, TLB). William James said, "Perhaps the greatest discovery of this century is that if you change your attitude, you can change your life."

It's passion that persuades. "Believing is seeing. It's much more effective than the old notion that seeing is believing" (Terrence Deal). Love the thing you do and you will keep doing better and bigger things.

NUGGET #15

If You Don't Do It, You Don't Really Believe It.

People judge you by your actions, not your intentions. You may have a heart of gold, but so does a hard boiled egg" (*Good Reading*). A thousand words will not leave so lasting an impression as one deed. Action is the natural fruit of direction. Make your good intentions always followed by appropriate actions. If you don't do it, you don't really believe it. "If ye *know* these things, happy are ye if you *do* them" (John 13:17, italics added).

Prayer should never be an excuse for inaction. Sometimes, I believe that the Lord speaks to us like he did Moses when He said: "Quit praying and get the people moving! Forward march!" (Ex. 14:15, TLB). Most prayers are only going to be answered when you attach action to them.

Some people spend their whole time searching for what's right, but they can't seem to find any time to practice it. "Remember, too, that knowing what is right to do and then not doing it is sin" (James 4:17, TLB). Your life story is not written with a pen, but with your actions. To *do* nothing is the way to *be* nothing.

"There is no idleness without a thousand troubles" (Welsh proverb). The devil's number one tool is not an active sinner, but an inactive Christian. "The devil tempts some, but an idle man tempts the devil" (English proverb). Be sure to keep busy doing what's right so that the devil may always find you occupied.

Action subdues fear. When we challenge our fears, we master them. When we wrestle with our problems, they lose their grip on us. When we dare to confront the things that scare us, we open the door to our liberty.

Momentum doesn't just happen. "The common conception is that motivation leads to action, but the reverse is true—action precedes motivation" (Robert McKain). "Don't wait to be motivated. Take the bull by the horns until you have him screaming for mercy" (Michael Cadena).

Laziness is a load. Nothing is more exhausting than searching for easy ways to make a living. Laziness keeps on and on, but soon enough it arrives at poverty. We are weakest when we try to get something for nothing. "Hard work brings prosperity; playing around brings poverty" (Prov. 28:19, TLB).

A man of words and not of deeds is like a flower bed full of weeds. Don't let weeds grow around your dreams. To only dream of the person you would like to be is to waste the person you are. Some men dream of great accomplishments, while others stay awake and do them. Henry Ford once commented: "You can't build a reputation on what you're going to do." "Shun idleness. It is a rust that attaches itself to the most brilliant of metals" (Voltaire).

We need to be like a cross between a carrier pigeon and a woodpecker: he not only carries the message, but he also knocks on the door.

NUGGET #16

You Cannot Find Until You Define.

Opportunity is all around you. What matters is where you put your focus. Ask yourself this question every day: "Where should my focus be?" Where you focus your attention, you create strength and momentum.

These are the characteristics of momentum: 1) it is single-minded; 2) it is unwavering in the pursuit of a goal; 3) it has passion which knows no limits; 4) it demands a concentrated intensity and a definite sense of destiny; and, most of all, 5) it has a boundless vision and commitment to excellence.

Concentration is the key that opens the door to accomplishment. "The first law of success...is concentration—to bend all the energies to one point, and to go directly to that point, looking neither to the right nor to the left" (William Mathews). The most successful people have always been those of concentration, who have struck their blows in one place until they have accomplished their purpose. They are of one specific idea, one steady aim, one single and concentrated purpose.

What a great disparity there is between some people's dreams and the results they achieve! It is due to the difference in their commitment to bring together all the options of their ability and to focus them upon one point.

There are two quick ways to disaster: taking nobody's advice and taking everybody's advice. Learn to say no to the good so you can say yes to the best. A.P. Goethe says there are three strategies for success: " 1) a big waste basket—you must know what to eliminate;

2) know what to preserve; 3) know when to say no, for developing the power to say no gives us the capacity to say yes."

We accomplish things by directing our desires, not by ignoring them. What an immense power you will have over your life when you possess distinct aims. Your words, the tone of your voice, your dress, your very motions change and improve when you begin to live for a reason.

Don't be a person who is uncertain about the future and hazy about the present. Stay in the groove without making it a rut. Make something your specialty. Even God, who is God, cannot please everyone, so don't you try. You cannot find until you define. To finish the race, stay on the track.

I am astonished at the aimlessness of most people's lives and how easily they delegate the direction of their lives to others. "Learn to define yourself, to content yourself with some specific thing and some definite work; dare to be what you really are, and to learn to accept with good grace all that you are not"(Anonymous).

NUGGET #17

Impatience Is One Big "Get-Ahead-Ache."

"Time sure changes things," an airline passenger told his companion. "When I was a boy I used to sit in a flat bottom rowboat and fish in the lake down there below us. Every time a plane flew over, I'd look up and wish I were in it. Now I look down and wish I were fishing." Timing sure does change things.

Being at the right place at the right time makes all the difference. How important is timing? Theodore Roosevelt said, "Nine-tenths of wisdom is being wise in time."

The fact that you're reading this book shows that you want to grow—to get somewhere. Like most of us, you want to get there as fast as you can. But, keep in mind that too swift is as untimely as too slow. The situation that seems urgent seldom is. Haste slows every dream and opens the door to failure. "The more haste, the less speed" (John Heywood).

It's more important to know where you're going, than to see how fast you can get there. "Impatient people always get there too late" (Jean Dutourd). We undo ourselves by impatience.

One of the most frequent causes for the failure of able-bodied men is impatience in waiting for results. "The haste of a fool is the slowest thing in the world" (Thomas Shadwell). Whoever is in a hurry shows that the thing he is doing is too big for him. Impatience is one big "get-ahead-ache."

"There is a time to let things happen and a time to make things happen" (Hugh Prather). That's what Ecclesiastes 3:1 means when it says "To everything there is a season, and a time to every purpose

47

under the heaven." Life is lived in seasons, which means we are to do different things at different times. Do the right thing at the right time. A Chinese proverb says, "Never leave your field in spring or your house in winter." God never sends a winter without following it with the joy of spring, the growth of summer and the harvest of fall.

Be a good finisher and never claim a victory prematurely. The greatest assassin of dreams is haste, the desire to reach things before the right time.

NUGGET #18

Momentum Makers.

1. Choice

2. Commitment

3. Dreams

4. Faith

5. Prayer

6. Action

7. Focus

8. Small steps

9. Listening

10. Creativity

11. Standing alone

12. Wisdom

13. Zeal

14. Purpose

15. Positioning

16. Talents

17. The Word

18. Right friends

19. Change

20. Forgiveness

21. Pure heart

22. Right spirit

23. Excellence

24. Thanksgiving

25. Love

26. Persistence

27. Giving

28. Priorities

29. Risk

30. Vision

31. Compassion

32. Obedience

33. Servanthood

34. Yieldedness

35. Joy

36. Honesty

37. Character

NUGGET #19

Stay Out Of Your Own Way.

Here's the first rule of winning: Don't beat yourself. The biggest enemy is you. When you find yourself getting in your own way, you're acting like an old refrigerator–it slowly builds an ice formation which, if allowed to accumulate unchecked, will reduce its effectiveness considerably.

"I have never met a man who has given me as much trouble as myself" (Dwight L. Moody). The first and best victory is to conquer yourself. All of the significant battles are waged within one's self.

Very often a change of self is needed more than a change of scene. Here's some good advice: "Only you can hold yourself back; only you can stand in your own way...only you can help yourself. There is no one to stop you but yourself.

When you find yourself standing in your own way, you'll always hope vaguely and dread precisely. Talk back to your internal critic. "If you want to move your greatest obstacle, realize that your obstacle is yourself–and that the time to act is now" (Nido Cubein).

You must begin to think of yourself as becoming the person you want to be. "Give the man you'd like to be a look at the man you are" (Edgar Guest). Change what you tell yourself. "No one really knows enough to be a pessimist" (Norman Cousins).

Remember, "One of the nice things about problems is that a good many of them do not exist except in our imaginations" (Steve Allan). The fear you fear is mostly within yourself and nowhere else.

There are two forces warring against each other within us. One says you can't, the other says with God you can. "It's not the mountain we conquer, but ourselves" (Sir Edmond Hillary). The basic problem most people have is that they are doing nothing to solve their basic problem. This problem is, they build a case against themselves.

"Stay out of your own way" (David Blunt).

LOOKING OUTWARD

NUGGET #20

Paths Without Obstacles Don't Lead Anywhere.

To get to the promised land, you'll have to navigate your way through the wilderness. All of us encounter obstacles, problems and challenges across our paths. How we respond to them and view them is one of the most important decisions that we make. Look at what the Bible says about them: "Dear brothers, is your life full of difficulties and temptations? Then be happy, for when the way is rough, your patience has a chance to grow. So let it grow, and don't try to squirm out of your problems. For when your patience is finally in full bloom, then you will be ready for anything, strong in character, full and complete" (James 1:2-4, TLB).

A man with twenty challenges is twice as alive as a man with ten. If you haven't got any challenges, you should get down on your knees and ask, "Lord, don't You trust me anymore?" So what if you've got problems. That's good! Why? Because consistent victories over your problems are the steps on your stairway to success. Be thankful for problems, for if they were less difficult, someone with less ability would have your job.

"A successful man will never see the day that does not bring a fresh quota of problems, and the mark of success is to deal with them effectively" (Lauris Norstad). James Bilkey observed, "You will never be the person you can be if pressure, tension and discipline are taken out of your life." Refuse to let yourself become discouraged by temporary setbacks. If you are beginning to encounter some hard bumps, don't worry. At least you are out of a rut. Circumstances are not your master.

You can always measure a man by the amount of opposition it takes to discourage him. When the water starts to rise, you can too. You can go over, not under. Bernie Siegal wrote, "Obstacles across our path can be spiritual flat tires—disruptions in our lives seem to be disastrous at the time, but end by redirecting our lives in a meaningful way."

The truth is, if you find a path with no obstacles, it is probably a path that doesn't lead to anywhere important. Man's adversity is always God's opportunity. Adversity gives birth to opportunity. Jesus said, "In this world you will have trouble. But take heart! I have overcome the world" (John 16:33, NIV).

"What is the difference between an obstacle and an opportunity? Our attitude towards it. Every opportunity has a difficulty, and every difficulty has an opportunity," said J. Sidlo Baxter. Lou Holtz says, "Show me someone who has done something worthwhile, and I'll show you someone who has overcome adversity." Many people have good intentions, but then something bad happens and they simply stop. Every path has a puddle, but those puddles can be God telling us where to step.

Remember, the travel is worthy of the travail when you're on the right road. If you would just recognize that life is difficult, things would be much easier for you. Norman Vincent Peale pointed out, "Every problem has in it the seeds of its own solution. If you don't have any problems, you don't get any seeds." Watch out for emergencies. They are your big chance! Live your life so that you can say, "I've had a life full of challenges, thank God!"

NUGGET #21

Don't Measure Yourself With Another Man's Coat.

"**E**very man must do two things alone," said Martin Luther. "He must do his own believing and his own dying." When you compare yourself with others, you will become bitter or vain for always there will be greater and lesser persons than yourselves. Making comparisons is a sure path to frustration. But comparison is never proof. "You can't clear your own fields while counting the rocks on your neighbor's farm" (Joan Welch). "The grass may be greener on the other side of the fence, but there's probably more of it to mow" (Lois Cory). Hills look small and green a long way off.

What a waste of energy, time and effort when you compare your place and plan with that of other people. I was amazed recently when I heard from a friend that I hadn't heard from for three to four years. He told me that he felt worse about his life because of some things I had accomplished. I couldn't help but be perplexed at his comments, and I asked him, "Do you mean that you would have felt a lot better if I'd done horribly the last three to four years?" Well, of course he said no. Success in someone else's life does not hurt the chances for success in yours.

Life is more fun when you don't keep score for others. Success really is simply a matter of doing what you do best and not worrying about what the other person is going to do. You carry success or failure within yourself. It does not depend on outside conditions.

Ask yourself this question that Earl Nightingale posed: "Are you motivated by what you really want out of life, or are you mass-motivated?" Make sure you decide what you really want, not what someone else wants for you. Do you say, "I'm good, but not as good as I ought to be," or do you say, "I'm not as bad as a lot of other people?" The longer you dwell on another's weakness, the more you affect your own mind with unhappiness. You must create your own system and your own plan, or you will be enslaved by another man's.

Every person who trims himself to suit everybody will soon find himself whittled away. You are only supposed to compare your place and plan with God's will for your life.

If a thousand people say a foolish thing, it is still a foolish thing. Direction from God is never a matter of public opinion. A wise man makes his own decision; an ignorant man follows public opinion. Don't think you're necessarily on the right road because it's a well-beaten path. The greatest risk in life is to wait for and depend on others for your security. Don't measure yourself with another man's coat. Don't judge yourself through someone else's eyes.

NUGGET #22

Invest In Others.

One of the most exciting decisions you can make is to decide to be on the lookout for opportunities to invest in others. For me, this has been one of the most powerful principles of momentum that I've implemented in my life. About ten years ago, I remember driving to Tulsa, Oklahoma, from St. Louis with my family. I was listening to a Zig Ziglar tape and on this tape he said, "You'll always have everything you want in life if you'll help enough other people get what they want." When I heard this statement, literally, something went off inside of me, and I said out loud, "I'm going to do it." That decision to look for ways to help others, to invest in them, changed my life.

I believe that one of the marks of true greatness is to develop greatness in others. "There are three keys to more abundant living: caring about others, daring for others and sharing with others" (William Ward). I have found that really great men have a unique perspective. That perspective is that greatness is not deposited in them to stay but rather to flow through them into others. "We make a living by what we get, but we make a life by what we give" (Norman MacEwan). Assign yourself the purpose of making others happy and thereby give yourself a gift.

People have a way of becoming what you encourage them to be. Ralph Waldo Emerson observed: "Trust men and they will be true to you; treat them greatly and they will show themselves great." Spend your life lifting people up, not putting people down. Goethe advised: "Treat people as if they were what they ought to be and help them to become what they are capable of being."

Whatever we praise, we increase. There is no investment you can make that will pay you so well as the effort to scatter sunshine and good cheer into others throughout your journey. "The person who renders loyal service in a humble capacity will be chosen for higher responsibilities, just as the biblical servant who multiplied the one pound given by his master was made ruler over ten cities" (B. C. Forbes).

There are two types of people in the world: those who come into a room and say, "Here I am!" and those who come in and say, "Ah, there you are!" How do you know a good man? A good man makes others good. Find happiness by helping others find it.

"What you make happen for others, God will make happen for you" (Mike Murdock). The Bible says it this way: "Knowing that whatsoever good thing any man doeth, the same shall he receive of the Lord" (Eph. 6:8). A good deed bears interest. You cannot hold a light to another's path without brightening your own. Develop greatness in others.

"There is no more noble occupation in the world than to assist another human being—to help someone succeed" (Allan McGinnis). "The true meaning of life is to plant trees under whose shade you do not expect to sit" (Nelson Henderson). The greatest use of your life is to spend it for something and on someone that will outlast it. "If you cannot win, make the one ahead of you break the record" (Jan McKeithen). Invest in others. It pays great dividends.

NUGGET #23

You Don't Learn Anything While You're Talking.

One of the best ways to persuade others is to listen to them. You'll find that a gossip talks to you about others, a bore talks to you about himself and a brilliant conversationalist talks to you about yourself and then listens to your reply. You don't learn anything while you're talking. The truth is that the more you say the less people remember.

"Keep your mouth closed and you'll stay out of trouble" (Prov. 21:23, TLB). A man is known by the silence he keeps. Don't miss many valuable opportunities to hold your tongue and listen to what the other person is saying. When you have nothing to say, say nothing. Silence is a friend who will never betray you.

The greatest skill you can develop is the skill of listening to others. "The man of few words and settled mind is wise; therefore, even a fool is thought to be wise when he is silent. It pays him to keep his mouth shut" (Prov. 17:27-28, TLB).

Talk is cheap because supply exceeds demand. "As you go through life, you are going to have many opportunities to keep your mouth shut. Take advantage of all of them" (West Virginia Gazette). There must have been some reason God made man's ears to stay open and his mouth to be shut. As a man grows older and wiser, he talks less and says more.

Learn to listen. Sometimes opportunity knocks very softly. You will find that God will speak for the man who holds his peace. There is only one rule for being a good talker: learn to listen.

Be a good listener. Too much talk will always include error. Your ears will never get you in trouble. One of the most powerful principles you can implement in your life is the principle of listening to others. Proverbs 10:19 says: "Don't talk so much. You keep putting your foot in your mouth. Be sensible and turn off the flow!" (TLB).

NUGGET #24

Don't Let Things Stick To You.

As I have had the privilege of meeting hundreds of people over the past several years, one thing that always stands out to me is how many people have things attached to them. For example, people allow a critical statement made by a third-grade teacher, a failure or mistake made ten or fifteen years ago or the comments of a negative neighbor last week hold them back from their destiny. It is a foolish man that adheres to all that he hears. Not everyone has a right to speak into your life. Not every word requires an answer. One of the most powerful principles that you can apply to acquire momentum is the principle of not letting things stick to you.

I really believe that one of the major benefits of asking forgiveness from God is that things no longer "stick to us." He says that if we confess our sins He is faithful and just to forgive us of our sins. But incredibly, God doesn't stop there (and that would be great enough), but He also promises to cleanse us from all unrighteousness (See 2 Pet. 2:13). When He cleanses us from all unrighteousness, He gives us a right standing before the Father. Why? He doesn't want things to stick to us. When we have received a right standing before the Father, we are free of the failures and mistakes, wrong words and attitudes of the past, and we are released and free to accomplish things for the future.

Don't worry if you don't get what you think you should. What seems so necessary today might not even be desirable tomorrow.

Paul Harvey was right when he said, "In times like these, it helps to recall that there have always been times like these." If we can forget our troubles as easily as we forget our blessings, how different things would be.

One way to be free of things that want to stick to you is to take your mind off the things that seem to be against you. Thinking about these negative factors simply builds into them a power that they truly don't possess. Talking about your grievances merely adds to those grievances.

Attach yourself to God's forgiveness, plan and Word. Then watch yourself become loosed from former "sticky" situations.

NUGGET #25

Be The First To Forgive.

L iving a life of unforgiveness is like leaving the parking brake on when you drive your car. It causes you to slow down and lose your momentum. One of the most expensive luxuries that you can possess is unforgiveness toward someone. A deep-seated grudge in your life eats away at your peace of mind like a deadly cancer, destroying a vital organ of life. In fact, there are few things as pathetic and terrible to behold as the person who has harbored a grudge and hatred for many years.

The heaviest load that you can possibly carry on your back is a pack of grudges. So if you want to travel far and fast, then travel light. Unpack all of your envies, jealousies, unforgiveness, revenges and fears.

Never reject forgiveness or the opportunity to forgive. The weak can never forgive because forgiveness is a characteristic of the strong. When you live a life of unforgiveness, revenge naturally follows. But revenge is the deceiver. It looks sweet, but it's most often bitter. It always costs more to avenge a wrong than to bear it. You never can win by trying to even the score.

Be the first to forgive. Forgiveness can be your deepest need and highest achievement. Without forgiveness, life is governed by an endless cycle of resentment and retaliation. What a dreadful waste of effort. "He who has not forgiven an enemy has never yet tasted one of the most sublime enjoyments of life," declares Johann Lavater.

Forgiving those who have wronged you is a key to personal peace. What the world needs is that peace that passes all misunderstanding. Forgiveness releases you for action and freedom.

Never cut what can be untied. Don't burn bridges. You'll be surprised how many times you have to cross over that same river. Unforgiveness is empty, but forgiveness makes a future possible. You'll "start your day on the right foot" if you ask yourself everyday, "Who do I need to forgive?"

NUGGET #26

There Are Million-Dollar Ideas Around You Every Day.

Sometimes as I drive down different parts of the city where I live, I can't help but notice the vast variety of businesses. Many times I pause and think, "That's someone's dream; that's someone's unique idea; that's someone's million-dollar opportunity." I believe there are significant opportunities and ideas around us every day. In fact, Ralph Waldo Emerson said, "God hides things by putting them near us."

The best opportunities and ideas are hidden near you. The Bible says, "The earth is full of the goodness of the Lord" (Ps. 33:5). You can see a thousand miracles around you every day, or you can see nothing. Your big opportunity may be right where you are now.

There are no limits to your possibilities. At any moment you have more possibility than you can act upon. Too many people spend their whole lives devoted to only solving problems and not recognizing opportunities.

Where do you hear opportunity knocking, and how can you answer that knock? Charles Fillmore answered, "There are always opportunities everywhere, just as there always have been." Earl Nightingale said, "You are, at this moment, standing right in the middle of your own `acres of diamonds.'" He also pointed out, "Wherever there is danger, there lurks opportunity; wherever there is opportunity, there lurks danger. The two are inseparable. They go together."

A successful person "always has a number of projects planned, to which he looks forward. Any one of them could change the course of his life overnight" (Mark Caine). Opportunities? They are all around us. There are opportunities laying dormant everywhere waiting for the observant eye to discover. Look at the same thing as everyone else, but see something different.

The stars are constantly shining, but we often do not see them until dark hours. The same is true with opportunities. It is true what Pogo said, "Gentlemen, we're surrounded by insurmountable opportunities."

NUGGET #27

Momentum Breakers.

1. Indecision

2. Complaining

3. Fear

4. Worry

5. Regret

6. Obstacles

7. The past

8. Alibis

9. Excuses

10. Tradition

11. Envy

12. Criticism

13. Wrong friends

14. Mistakes

15. Unforgiveness

16. Procrastination

17. Distractions

18. Lying

19. Quitting

20. Double-mindedness

21. Hesitation

22. Talking

23. Failures

24. Delay

25. Jealousy

26. Impatience

27. Aimlessness

28. Disobedience

29. Strife

30. Misdirection

31. Conformity

32. Dishonesty

33. Ingratitude

34. Security

35. Lukewarmness

NUGGET #28

There Are Good Ships And Bad Ships, But The Best Ships Are Friendships.

Who you choose to be your closest friends or associates is one of the most important decisions you will make during the course of your life. "You are the same today that you are going to be in five years from now except for two things: the people with whom you associate and the books you read" (Charlie "Tremendous" Jones). The Bible says that if you associate with wise men you'll become wise, but a companion of fools will be destroyed (see Prov. 13:20). You will become like those with whom you closely associate.

"Friends in your life are like pillars on your porch: Sometimes they hold you up; sometimes they lean on you; sometimes it's just enough to know they're standing by" (Anonymous). "Iron sharpeneth iron; so a man sharpeneth the countenance of his friend" (Prov. 27:17). A real friend is a person who, when you've made a fool of yourself, lets you forget it. Good friendship always multiplies our joy and divides our grief.

I've found that the best friends are those who bring out the best in you. A true friend is someone who is there for you when they'd rather be somewhere else. "A friend loveth at all times, and a brother is born for adversity" (Prov. 17:17). I believe that we should keep our friendships in constant repair.

A good friend never gets in your way unless you're on your way down. A good friend is one who walks in when others walk out. The right kind of friends are those with whom you can dare to be yourself. A friend is one before whom you can dream aloud. For me, my best friends are those who understand my past, believe in my future and accept me today just the way I am.

The wrong kind of friends, unlike the good kind of friends, bring out the worst—not the best—in you. You know the kind I'm talking about. They are the persons who absorb sunshine and radiate gloom. There are people who will always come up with reasons why you can't do what you want. Ignore them. The Bible says in Proverbs 25:19, "Putting confidence in an unreliable man is like chewing with a sore tooth, or trying to run on a broken foot" (TLB). A day away from the wrong associations is like a month in the country. Mark Twain wrote: "Keep away from people who try to belittle your ambitions. Small people always do that, but the really great make you feel that you, too, can become great." Never have a companion who casts you in the shade.

A true friend doesn't sympathize with your weakness—he helps summon your strength. Associations are based on the same interests or mutual problems. Be sure you know the difference.

A friend is someone who knows all about you but likes you anyway. "Treat your friends as you do your best pictures, and place them in their best light" (Jennie Churchill). A true friend will see you through when others see that you're through. Friends communicate at a heart level. There are good ships and there are bad ships, but the best ships are friendships.

NUGGET #29

Dig For Diamonds, Don't Chase Butterflies.

One of the devil's primary strategies to hinder our momentum is to use distractions to keep us from being focused on the plan that God has for us. Determine what you really want and what God wants for you. This will keep you from chasing butterflies and put you to work digging for diamonds.

Pay more attention to the things that are working positively in your life than to the things that are giving you trouble. Too many times people devote the majority of their effort, time and attention to those things that are never going to be productive in their lives. "If a man could have half his wishes, he would double his troubles," said Ben Franklin.

Clear your mind of the things that are out of your control in order to focus on and act upon your goals of the day. You'll always get lost by trying to find an alternate route for the straight and narrow. "He will keep in perfect peace all those who trust in him, whose thoughts turn often to the Lord!" (Is. 26:3, TLB). "Life's greatest tragedy is to lose God and not miss Him" (F. W. Norwood).

The words of others will be one of the primary distractions that will try to hinder you. Do just once what others say you can't do and you will never pay attention to their limitations again. If you let other people stop you, they will.

When you let yourself be distracted by the fear and doubt that others want to bring in your life, you will have a quick ear for bad news and large eyes for trouble ahead. You'll be a great inventor of things that will never happen. Jesus said, "Anyone who lets himself be distracted from the work I plan for him is not fit for the Kingdom of God" (Luke 9:62, TLB).

Concentrate on one thing at a time and rule out all influences that don't have bearing on the task at hand. Said George Bernard Shaw: "People are always blaming their circumstances for what they are. I don't believe in circumstances. The people who get on in this world are the people who get up and look for circumstances they want, and, if they can't find them, make them." Within your concentration the rest of the world cannot distract you. "Look straight ahead; don't even turn your head to look. Watch your step. Stick to the path and be safe" (Prov. 4:25-26, TLB).

NUGGET #30

Nothing Great Is Created Suddenly.

One of the most common prayers I pray for others (and myself) is this: "Lord, please send small opportunities across their paths to do what you've called them to do." When we're faithful in those small opportunities God says to us, "You have been faithful in handling this small amount...so now I will give you many more responsibilities. Begin the joyous tasks I have assigned to you" (Matt. 25:21, TLB).

People who think they are too big to do little things are perhaps too little to be asked to do big things. Small opportunities are often the beginning of great enterprises.

Nothing great is created suddenly. Nothing can be done except little by little. Never decide to do nothing just because you can only do a little. Within that little thing lies a big opportunity. Small things make a big difference; therefore, do all that it takes to be successful in little things.

You will never do great things if you can't do small things in a great way. All difficult things have their beginning in that which is easy, and great things in that which is small. One of the major differences between people who have momentum and those who don't, is that those that do, pay attention to their small ideas and opportunities.

The courage to begin is the same courage it takes to succeed. That courage separates dreamers from achievers. The beginning is the most important part of any endeavor. Worse than a quitter is the man who is afraid to begin. Ninety percent of success is showing up and starting. You may be disappointed if you fail, but you are doomed if you don't try.

Don't be deceived: knowledge of a path can never be a substitute for putting one foot in front of the other. Discover step by step excitement. Robert Schuller sums it up: "Winning starts with beginning." The first step is the hardest. "That's why many fail—because they don't get started—they don't go. They don't overcome inertia. They don't begin" (W. Clement Stone).

Dare to begin. No endeavor is worse than that which is not attempted. You don't know what you can do until you have tried. People, like trees, must grow or wither. There's no standing still. Do what you can. "It is always your next move" (N. Hill).

NUGGET #31

No Person Is More Cheated Than The Selfish Man.

The way to grow is to give. Here is a simple but powerful principle: Always give people more than they expect. "And whosoever shall compel thee to go a mile, go with him twain" (Matt. 5:41). Give more than they expect and do it cheerfully. "If there be any truer measure of a man than by what he does, it must be by what he gives" (Robert South).

It's a universal law: we have to give before we get. In giving to others you'll find yourself blessed. The giver's harvest is always full. To get, give. Getters don't get –givers get. When you give of yourself, you'll receive more than you give.

We tire of those pleasures we take but never of those we give. The person who sows seeds of kindness will have a perpetual harvest. Be kinder than necessary. Kindness is a hard thing to give away. It keeps coming back to the giver. Proverbs 11:17 says: "Your own soul is nourished when you are kind; it is destroyed when you are cruel" (TLB).

One great way to give is in words of appreciation. A compliment is like verbal sunshine. "How forcible are right words!" (Job 6:25). So never be sparing with giving words of appreciation, especially when they are deserved by those around you. Everyone loves praise. Look hard for ways to give it to them. The good words you give are worth so much and cost so little.

That which you cannot give away, you do not possess. It possesses you. Remember, what you give will bring you more pleasure than what you get. If you are selfish, you'll find yourself bounded on the north, south, east and west by just yourself. No man is more cheated than the selfish man.

God is a giver. So be like Him and do good to everyone. Be ready to give in an instant because when you give soon, it's like giving twice. Giving can become a good habit.

"The man who will use his skill and constructive imagination to see how much he can give for a dollar instead of how little he can give for a dollar, is bound to succeed" (Henry Ford).

NUGGET #32

Pick A Problem Bigger Than You.

People nearly always pick a problem their own size and ignore or leave to others the bigger or smaller ones. Pick a problem bigger than you. "Success - real success - in any endeavor demands more from an individual than most people are willing to offer–not more than they are capable of offering" (James Roche).

The desire for safety stands against every great and virtuous dream. Security is the first step towards stagnation. The trouble with this world is that too many people try to go through life with a catcher's mitt on both hands.

Boldness in vision is the first, second and third most important thing. He who dares nothing should expect nothing. "One who is contented with what he has done will never be famous for what he will do" (Christian Bovee). If you have achieved all you have planned for yourself, you have not planned enough.

Be used for a mighty purpose. Dare to do what's right for you. Choose a goal for which you are willing to exchange a piece of your life. The surest way to happiness is to lose yourself in a cause greater than yourself. You'll be unhappy if you do not reach for something beyond yourself.

"It is difficult to say what is impossible, for the dream of yesterday is the hope of today and the reality of tomorrow" (Robert Goddard). Every great action is impossible when it is undertaken. Only after it has become accomplished does it seem possible to the average man. To small thinkers, everything looks like a mountain.

The grandest things are, in some ways, the easiest to do because there is so little competition.

To be complacently satisfied with yourself is a sure sign that progress is about to end. If you are satisfied with yourself, you'd better change your ideals. "How much better to know that we have dared to live our dreams than to live our lives in a lethargy of regret" (Gilbert Caplin). "Moderation is a fatal thing. Nothing succeeds like excess" (Oscar Wilde).

You'll never succeed beyond your wildest dreams unless you have some wild dreams.

NUGGET #33

What Works? Work On That.

Everyone who got where he is had to begin where he was. Only one person in a thousand knows how to really live in the present. Our problem is that we seldom think of what we have, but we usually think of what we lack.

The failure wishes he could do things that he can't do. He thinks little of what he can do. What you *can* do...you can *do*.

"We don't need more strength or more ability or greater opportunity. What we need to use is what we have" (Basil Walsh). People are always ignoring something they can do and trying to do something they can't. Learning new things won't help the person who isn't using what he already knows. Success means doing the best we can with what we have.

Norman Vincent Peale said: "We've all heard that we have to learn from our mistakes, but I think it is more important to learn from our successes. If you learn only from your mistakes, you are inclined to learn only errors." Some people spend their whole lives failing and never even notice.

The main thing that's wrong with doing nothing is that you never know when you are finished. When you are through improving, you're through. Use whatever you have been given, and more will come to you. Never leave well enough alone. "Opportunities multiply as they are seized; they die when neglected" (Anonymous). "Every ceiling, when reached becomes a floor upon which one walks and now can see a new ceiling. Every exit is an entry somewhere" (Tom Stoppard).

"You can't control the weather, but you can control the moral atmosphere that surrounds you. Why worry about things you can't control? Get busy controlling the things that depend upon you" (*In a Nutshell*). "A strong, successful man is not the victim of his environment. He creates favorable conditions" (Orsen Marden).

The guy who gets ahead is the guy who does more than is necessary—and keeps on doing it. No matter how rough the path, some forge ahead; no matter how easy the going, some lag behind. Begin somewhere; you cannot fulfill your destiny on what you intend to do.

The best way to better your lot is to do a lot better. Build on the lot in life that you've been given.

NUGGET #34

Don't Belittle...Be Big.

People with momentum all have one trait – they attract criticism. How you respond to that criticism will determine the rate of your momentum. The person who never steps on anybody's toes is probably standing still. I was reading a cover story on Billy Graham in *Time* magazine recently and was surprised to find in that article several criticisms of him from fellow ministers. I was reminded that all great men get great criticism. Learn to accept and expect the unjust criticisms for your great goals and accomplishments. Even Jesus was repeatedly criticized. If Jesus was criticized, surely Billy Graham, you and I will be also.

It can be beneficial to receive constructive criticism from those who have your best interests at heart and are of like mind, but you're not responsible to respond to those who don't. You're responsible to respond to God. "Throw out the mocker, and you will be rid of tension, fighting and quarrels" (Prov. 22:10, TLB). Don't replace time spent with a friend and give it to a critic. I like what Edward Gibbon said: "I never make the mistake of arguing with people for whose opinions I have no respect."

It's a thousand times easier to criticize than create. That's why critics are never problem solvers. Sticks and stones are thrown only at fruit bearing trees. "Any fool can criticize, condemn and complain, and most do" (Dale Carnegie). My feeling is that the person who says it cannot be done, should not interrupt the one who is doing it. Just remember, when you are kicked from behind, it must mean you are out in front. A Yiddish proverb says a critic is like the girl who can't dance so she says the band can't play.

Critics know the answers without having probed deep enough to know the questions. When threatened by miraculous truth, they respond with the "facts." "Don't let others spoil your faith and joy with their philosophies, their wrong and shallow answers built on men's thoughts and ideas, instead of on what Christ has said" (Col. 2:8, TLB).

"A critic is a man created to praise greater men than himself, but he is never able to find them" (Richard LeGallienne). The critic is convinced that the chief purpose of sunshine is to cast shadows. He doesn't believe anything, but he still wants you to believe him. He always knows the "price of everything and the value of nothing" (Oscar Wilde). Don't waste time responding to your critics, because you owe nothing to a critic.

Don't belittle—be big. Don't become a critic. "We have no more right to put our discordant states of mind into the lives of those around us and rob them of their sunshine and brightness than we have to enter their houses and steal their silverware" (Julia Seton). In criticizing others, remember that you will work overtime for no pay. "Wherein thou judgest another, thou condemnest thyself" (Rom. 2:1). Never throw mud. If you do, you may hit your mark, but you will have dirty hands. Don't be a cloud because you failed to become a star. "Give so much time to the improvement of yourself that you have no time to criticize others" (Optimist Creed). Spend your time and energy creating, not criticizing.

A good thing to remember,
A better thing to do,
Work with the construction gang,
Not the wrecking crew (Anonymous).

NUGGET #35

Envy Never Enriched Anyone.

Picture a runner in full stride. He speeds through a pack of contenders, but he begins to look at who he's running against. What is the inevitable conclusion to this scene? That runner will at least slow down and probably stumble. The same things will happen to us if we allow the distraction of envy to turn our head as we run the race God has set before us. Instead of breaking records we're now breaking momentum.

Envy shoots at others and wounds herself (English proverb). It is self-punishment. "The man who covets is always poor" (Claudian). Envy never enriched any man. "Of all the passions, jealousy is that which exacts the hardest service and pays the bitterest wages. Its service is to watch the success of our enemy; its wages, to be sure of it" (Charles Colton).

Envy is like biting a dog because the dog bit you. "A relaxed attitude lengthens a man's life; jealousy rots it away (Prov. 14:30, TLB). Like rust consumes iron, envy consumes itself. Envy drains the joy, satisfaction, and purpose out of living.

If allowed to grow, envy breeds hate and revenge. To be angry and to seek revenge is like praying to the devil. The Bible says; "Also, see that no one pays back evil for evil, but always try to do good to each other and to everyone else." Revenge converts a little right into a big wrong.

"It is not love that is blind, but jealousy" (Lawrence Durrell). Envy sees the sea but not the rocks. "When an envious man hears another praised, he feels himself injured" (English proverb). "Love looks through a telescope, envy through a microscope" (Josh

Billings). "Beware of covetousness: for a man's life consisteth not in the abundance of things which he possesseths" (Luke 12:15). Your life is too valuable to waste by wanting what others have. Covetousness is a thirst that is never quenched.

A man is wise who does not grieve for the things which he has not, but rejoices for those which he has. Continually compare what you want with what you have, and you'll be unhappy. Instead, compare what you deserve with what you have, and you'll be happy. Decide to stick with love. Envy is too great a burden to bear.

LOOKING
UPWARD

NUGGET #36

Count God's Blessings, Don't Discount Them.

Be aggressively thankful. When it comes to living, an important issue is whether you take things for granted or take them with gratitude. Thanksgiving is the attitude of a productive life. No duty is more urgent than that of returning thanks. The person who isn't thankful for what he's got isn't likely to be thankful for what he's going to get. Ingratitude never finishes.

"Attitudes sour in the life that is closed to thankfulness. Soon selfish attitudes take over, closing life to better things" (C. Neil Strait). The person who forgets the language of gratitude will never find himself on speaking terms with happiness. Thanksgiving, you will find, will create power in your life because it opens the generators of your heart to respond gratefully, to receive joyfully and to react creatively. William Ward spoke wisely: "There are three enemies of personal peace: regret over yesterday's mistakes, anxiety over tomorrow's problems and ingratitude for today's blessing."

Know that you are blessed. If you can't be satisfied with what you've reached, be thankful for what you've escaped. Thank God and count your blessings at every opportunity. The words *think* and *thank* come from the same Latin root. If we take time to *think* more, we will undoubtedly *thank* more.

I like what Dwight L. Moody said: "Be humble or you'll stumble." There's a relationship between pride and ingratitude. Henry Ward Beecher pointed out: "A proud man is seldom a grateful man, for he never thinks he gets as much as he deserves." Don't be a person who has a highly developed instinct for being unhappy. Instead, "be glad for all God is planning for you. Be patient in trouble, and prayerful always" (Rom. 12:12, TLB). The best rule is, whatever God gives, gratefully receive. If we spend our time thanking God for the good things, there won't be any time left to weep over the bad.

Find a hundred things to be thankful for today. As you do, I guarantee five creative ideas will spring forth out of the mental conversation you will have with yourself. One of the most creative ways to generate momentum and opportunities is to sit down and write a thank-you note to fifty people who have influenced your life.

Our real prosperity lies in being thankful. Appreciative words are one of the most powerful forces for good on the earth. Kind words don't cost much, yet they accomplish much. Count God's blessings; don't discount them. Pray this, "God, you've given so much to me, give me one more thing—a grateful heart."

NUGGET #37

You Can Never Trust God Too Much.

Many people believe in God, but not many believe God. One of the most incredible places that we can live our lives is in a continual position of believing God. "God made us, and God is able to empower us to do whatever He calls us to do. Denying that we can accomplish God's work is not humility; it is the worst kind of pride" (Warren Wiersbe).

The man who puts God first will find God with him right up to the last. "In everything you do, put God first, and he will direct you and crown your efforts with success" (Prov. 3:6, TLB). Unless it includes believing God, it is not worthy of being called God's direction, for every divine direction that we receive from God will include us believing in Him.

"God never made a promise that was too good to be true," said D. L. Moody. One of the great things about believing God is found in Luke 18:27: "The things which are impossible with men are possible with God." When you join together with Him in His plan, things that were impossible now become possible. The superior man seeks success in God. The small man seeks success in himself or others. You have never tapped God's resources until you have attempted the impossible.

You may trust the Lord too little, but you can never trust Him too much. With God's strength behind you, His love with you and His arms underneath you, you are more than sufficient for the days ahead of you. "God is on our side," Abraham Lincoln wrote, "But it is more important to know that we are on God's side."

The fact is that anyone who doesn't believe in miracles is not a realist. Look around. Nothing is more real than miracles. When you leave God out, you'll find yourself without any invisible means of support. Great things are achieved by those who dare to believe that God inside them is superior to circumstances.

To say "impossible" always puts you on the losing side. If you dream big, believe big and pray big, do you know what will happen? Big things! Most of the things worth doing in history were declared impossible before they were done. What is possible is our highest responsibility.

The way each day will look to you all starts with who you're looking to. Look to God. Believe God. When you believe God you will see an opportunity in every problem, not problems in the middle of every opportunity. Proverbs 16:3 is true when it says, "Commit to the Lord whatever you do, and your plans will succeed" (NIV). Joshua 1:9 also says, "Yes, be bold and strong! Banish fear and doubt! For remember, the Lord your God is with you wherever you go" (TLB).

All great things have God involved in them. Dare to go with God farther than you can see. If something is beneficial for you, God will put it within your reach. One psalm in the Bible says, "No good thing will he withhold from them that walk uprightly" (Ps. 84:11). Never undertake anything for which you wouldn't have the conviction to ask the blessing of heaven. A small man stands on others. A great man stands on God.

NUGGET #38

Live Truly And You Will Truly Live.

You can't make wrong work. Never chase a lie: if you leave it alone, it will run itself to death. Everything you add to the truth, you inevitably subtract from it. It's discouraging to think how people nowadays are more shocked by honesty than by deceit. But honesty is essential to society. Thomas Jefferson said, "Honesty is the first chapter of the book of wisdom."

"Those that think it is permissible to tell `white lies' soon grow colorblind" (Awson O'Malley). We punish ourselves with every lie and we reward ourselves with every right action. A lie will add to your troubles, subtract from your energy, multiply your difficulties and divide your effectiveness.

"Truth is always strong, no matter how weak it looks, and falsehood is always weak no matter how strong it looks" (Marcus Antioninus). Never view anything as an advantage to you that will make you break your word. In the war between falsehood and truth, falsehood wins the first battle, but truth wins the war. "If we live truly, we shall truly live," said Ralph Waldo Emerson.

Liars are never free. The Bible says, "You will know the truth, and the truth will set you free" (John 8:32, TLB). Horace Greeley observed: "The darkest hour of any man's life is when he sits down to plan how to get money without earning it." Instead, "refuse the evil, and choose the good" (Is. 7:15). "Dishonest gain will never last, so why take the risk?" (Prov. 21:6, TLB). The fact is that ill-gotten gain is always scattered by the devil.

When you stretch the truth, others can see through it. When you stretch the truth, watch out for the snap-back. Make your word your bond. Broken promises cause the world's greatest accidents. Honesty always lasts longest. A lie never lives to be old.

"It makes all the difference in the world whether we put truth in the first place or in the second place" (John Morley). As scarce as the truth is, the supply has always been in excess of the demand. Wrong is wrong no matter who does it or says it. Truth does not cease to exist because it is ignored, and it doesn't change depending on whether it is believed by a majority of people. The truth is always the strongest argument.

Truth exists. Only lies are invented. Truth shines in darkness. "There is never an instant's truce between virtue and vice. Goodness is the only investment that never fails" (Henry David Thoreau).

Truth needs no crutches. If it limps, it's a lie. A lie stands on one leg and a truth on two. Proverbs 11:3 says: "A good man is guided by his honesty; the evil man is destroyed by his dishonesty" (TLB). "You'll find that life is an uphill battle for the person who's not on the level" (Joan Welsh).

NUGGET #39

We're All In This Together — By Ourselves.

Every great idea and dream must be established between you and God alone. There will come times where only you and He will believe it is going to happen. Can you stand alone? There is power in the principle of standing alone and being alone.

John Gardner declared: "The cynic says, 'One man can't do anything.' I say, 'Only one man can do anything.'" Nobody can do it for you. No one will do it for you. Longfellow puts it this way: "Not in the clamor of the crowded streets, not in the shouts or plaudits of the throng, but in ourselves are triumph and defeat." You can't delegate your thinking, dreaming or believing to others.

Thomas Edison, who claimed he could think better because of his partial deafness, said: "The best thinking has been done in solitude. The worst has been done in turmoil." Even God declares: "Be still, and know that I am God" (Ps. 46:10).

Eagles fly alone; crows fly in groups. Know how to get away. Do not belong so completely to others that you do not belong to yourself. The fact is that we're all in this together—by ourselves.

Alexander Graham Bell made this observation: "Don't keep forever on the public road. Leave the beaten path occasionally and drive into the woods. You'll be certain to find something that you've never seen before. One discovery will lead to another, and before you know it, you will have something worth thinking about to occupy your mind."

A reasonable amount of time alone is indispensable, but it should primarily be time spent preparing to return to the battle. Be sure to spend some time alone on a regular basis.

Don't accept that others know you better than yourself. Great leaders have always encountered violent opposition from mediocre minds. The biggest mistake that you can make is to believe that you work for someone else. You really work for yourself and for God's plan for your life.

Learn to be alone and stand alone or nothing worthwhile will catch up to you.

NUGGET #40

Be Easily Satisfied With the Very Best.

Start every task thinking how to do it better than it has ever been done before. "Start a crusade in your life to dare to be your very best" (William Danforth). Become a yardstick of quality. Do the right thing regardless of what others think. Most people aren't used to an environment where excellence is expected.

"It is a funny thing about life; if you refuse to accept anything but the best, you very often get it" (Somerset Maughan). Think only of the best, work only for the best and expect only the best. Excellence is never an accident. "There is a way to do it better...find it" (Thomas Edison). There's always an excellent way of doing everything. "Hold yourself responsible for a higher standard than anybody else expects of you. Never excuse yourself" (Henry Ward Beecher).

"It is those who have this imperative demand for the best in their natures and those who will accept nothing short of it, that hold the banners of progress, that set the standards, the ideals for others" (Orsen Marden). "Happy is the man who doesn't give in and do wrong when he is tempted, for afterwards he will get as his reward the crown of life that God has promised those who love Him" (James 1:12, TLB). Excellence measures a man by the height of his ideals, the breadth of his compassion, the depth of his convictions and the length of his persistence. People will always determine your character by observing what you stand for, fall for and lie for.

Perfection, fortunately, is not the best alternative to mediocrity. A more sensible alternative is excellence. Striving for excellence rather than perfection is stimulating and rewarding; striving for perfection in practically anything is frustrating and futile. We are what we repeatedly do. Excellence, then, is not an act but a habit. "I advise you to obey only the Holy Spirit's instructions. He will tell you where to go and what to do, and then you won't always be doing the wrong things your evil nature wants you to do" (Gal. 5:16, TLB). Human excellence means nothing unless it works with the consent of God. "Excellence demands that you be better than yourself" (Ted Engstrom).

There is always a heavy demand for fresh mediocrity—don't give into it. Instead, be easily satisfied with the very best. For when you are delivering your very best, that is when you will feel most successful. Never sell your principles for popularity or you'll find yourself bankrupt in the worst way. Dare to be true to the best you know.

NUGGET #41

Measure Your Life By Its Donation, Not Duration.

"Nobody cares how much you know until they know how much you care" (John Cassis). Life is a lot like the game of tennis. Those who don't serve well end up losing. A man asked Dr. Carl Menninger, "What would you advise a person to do if he felt a nervous breakdown coming on?" Most people expected him to reply, "Consult a psychiatrist." To their astonishment he replied, "Lock up your house, go across the railroad tracks, find someone in need and do something to help that person."

"Never forget to be truthful and kind. Hold these virtues tightly. Write them deep within your heart" (Prov. 3:3-4, TLB). "Unless life is lived for others, it is not worthwhile" (Mother Teresa). "A self-centered life is totally empty, while an empty life allows room for God" (Tom Haggai). If you are dissatisfied with your lot in life, build a service station on it. A good way to forget your troubles is to help others out of theirs.

Serving others is never entirely unselfish, for the giver always receives. "Your own soul is nourished when you are kind; it is destroyed when you are cruel" (Prov. 11:17, TLB). Think about what questions you will be asked at the close of your life on earth. Nathan Schaeffer says, "The question will not be, 'How much have you got?' but, 'How much have you given?' Not, 'How much have you won?' but, 'How much have you done?' Not, 'How much have you saved?' but, 'How much have you sacrificed?' It will be, 'How much have you loved and served?' Not, 'How much were you honored?' "

"Selfishness is the greatest curse of the human race" (W. E. Gladstone). Self-interest is a fire that consumes others and then self. Since nine-tenths of our unhappiness is selfishness, think instead in terms of what the other person wants. It is literally true that you can succeed best and quickest by helping others succeed.

"The measure of life is not in its duration, but in its donation. Everyone can be great because everyone can serve" (Peter Marshall). When you are serving others, life is no longer meaningless. "One thing I know; the only ones among you who will really be happy are those who have sought and found how to serve" (Albert Schweitzer). You can't help another without helping yourself. "The liberal soul shall be made fat: and he that watereth, shall be watered also himself" (Prov. 11:25).

No one achieves greatness without being of service. Never reach out your hand unless you're willing to extend an arm. The roots of happiness grow deepest in the soil of service. Happiness is like potato salad—when shared with others, it's a picnic. If you want to know if you have a successful life, ask yourself if people would call you a servant.

NUGGET #42

Do Today What You Want To Postpone Until Tomorrow.

The devil's number one strategy to get you to fail is procrastination. Realize that now is the best time to be alive and productive. If you want to make an easy job seem difficult, just keep putting off doing it. "We're all fugitives, and the things we didn't do yesterday are the bloodhounds" (Prism). Said Joseph Newton, "A duty dodged is like a debt unpaid; it is only deferred and we must come back and settle the account at last." Work is the best thing ever invented for killing time.

What holds us back? "There are those of us who are always 'about' to live. We're waiting until things change, until there is more time, until we are less tired, until we get a promotion, until we settle down—until, until, until. It always seems that there is some major event that must occur in our lives before we begin living" (George Sheehan). *One* of these days is really *none* of these days. The "by and by" never comes. The person who desires, but doesn't act, breeds stagnation. You should always expect poison from standing water.

About the only thing that comes to a procrastinator is old age. Do today what you want to postpone until tomorrow. "Do not allow idleness to deceive you; for while you give him today, he steals tomorrow from you" (H. Crowquill). Nothing is so fatiguing as the eternal hanging-on of an uncompleted task. When you run in place, everyone will pass you by.

When a person gets into a habit of wasting time, they are sure to waste a great deal that does not belong to them. "One day, today, is worth two tomorrows" (Ben Franklin). What may be done at anytime will be done at no time. "Life is like a taxi, the meter keeps a-ticking whether you're getting somewhere or standing still" (Lou Erickson). The successful person does the thing that others never get around to. What the fool does in the end, the wise man does in the beginning.

Prolonged idleness paralyzes initiative. "Don't stand shivering upon the banks; plunge in at once and have it over with" (Sam Slick). Tomorrow is the busiest day of the week. If there's a hill to climb, don't think that waiting will make it any smaller.

A sluggard takes a hundred steps because he would not take one in due time. If possible, make the decision now, even if the action is in the future. A reviewed decision is usually better than one reached at the last moment. "The fool with all his other thoughts, has this also; he is always getting ready to live" (Epicurus). He who fiddles around seldom gets to lead the orchestra. There is danger in delay for it is always better to reap two days too soon than one day too late. Pity the man who waits until the last day.

"Tomorrow will I live," the fool does say; tomorrow itself is too late; the wise live yesterday" (Martial). "While the fool is enjoying the little he has, I will hunt for more. The way to hunt for more is to utilize your odd moments...the man who is always killing time is really killing his own chances in life" (Arthur Brisbane).

NUGGET #43

Give God The Same Place In Your Heart That He Has In The Universe.

The most frequent prayer I pray for myself is based on Psalm 51:10. I've found that this prayer has been a key to momentum in my own life. It says: "Create in me a clean heart, Oh God; and renew a right spirit within me." There is a supernatural confidence, expectancy and peace that comes when we have a clean heart and a right spirit before the Father.

"The righteous shall move onward and forward; those with pure hearts shall become stronger and stronger" (Job 17:9, TLB). A pure heart will bring increased strength to your life. Keep your heart right, especially when it's sorely wounded.

Do what's right. If you don't want the fruit of sin, then stay out of the devil's orchard. No one can be caught in a place he does not visit. Unchecked evil grows. Evil that is tolerated will poison you and all those that you care about.

Just be honest with yourself. That, in itself, opens many doors for God to move in your heart and spirit. Admit where evil might lead you, and then do what you have to do to stay free. Keep your heart pure and be blessed. Jesus Christ says, "Blessed are the pure in heart" (Matt. 5:8). The Bible also says, "Be strong, and let your heart take courage, all you who hope in the Lord" (Ps. 31:24, NAS).

Keep true, never be ashamed of doing right; decide on what you think is right and stick to it. Hope, faith and a right spirit will literally starve despair. Despair is not handled by giving in. It is handled best by giving out. It's nice to be important, but it's always more important to be nice.

No power in the world can keep a first-class man down or a third-class man up. There is always a high cost to low living. Give God the place of supremacy in your heart that He holds in the universe. Allow Him to create a clean heart and right spirit in you. This will cause you to be a person of pure motives and a right attitude.

NUGGET #44

It Is Never Safe To Look Into The Future With Eyes Of Fear.

The worst liars in the world are your own fears. "Worry is the traitor in our camp that dampens our powder and weakens our aim" (William Jorden). William Ward showed the difference between faith and worry. "Worry is faith in the negative, trust in the unpleasant, assurance of disaster and belief in defeat...Worry is a magnet that attracts negative conditions. Faith is a more powerful force that creates positive circumstances...Worry is wasting today's time to clutter up tomorrow's opportunities with yesterday's troubles" (William A. Ward).

"Don't worry about anything; instead, pray about everything; tell God your needs and don't forget to thank him for his answers" (Phil. 4:6, TLB). "Let him have all your worries and cares, for he is always thinking about you and watching everything that concerns you" (1 Pet. 5:7, TLB).

Never make a decision based on fear. Worry comes when human beings interfere with God's plan for their lives. Don't ever find yourself giving something the "benefit of the doubt"—doubt has no benefit.

What causes most battles to be lost is the unfounded fear of the enemy's strength. A. Purnell Bailey says worry is like a fog: "The Bureau of Standards in Washington tells us that a dense fog covering seven city blocks, one hundred feet deep, is comprised of something less than one glass of water. That amount of water is divided into some 60,000,000 tiny drops. Not much there! Yet when these minute particles settle down over the city or countryside, they can blot out practically all vision. A cup full of worry does just about the same thing. We forget to trust God. The tiny drops of fretfulness close around our thoughts and we are submerged without vision."

One of the great discoveries you can make is to find that you can do what you were afraid you couldn't do. Fear and self-satisfaction lock men's minds against fresh ideas. When men are ruled by fear, they find themselves unable to make the very changes that will eliminate it.

Dale Carnegie wrote: "An old man was asked what had robbed him of joy in his life. His reply was, `Things that never happened.'" Do you remember the things you were worrying about a year ago? How did they work out? Didn't you waste a lot of energy on account of most of them? Didn't most of them turn out to be all right after all?"

"God never built a Christian strong enough to carry today's duties and tomorrow's anxieties piled on top of them" (Theodore Ledyard Cuyler). The psalmist found the best way to combat fear. "But when I am afraid, I will put my confidence in you. Yes, I will trust the promises of God. And since I am trusting him, what can mere man do to me?" (Ps. 56:3-4, TLB).

NUGGET #45

If God Is Your Father, Please Call Home.

Prayer brings momentum. It lifts the heart above the challenges of life and gives it a view of God's resources of victory and hope. Prayer provides power, poise, and peace for a person's purpose, plans and pursuits. The most powerful energy anyone can generate is prayer energy. Corre ten Boom said, "The devil smiles when we make plans. He laughs when we get too busy. But he trembles when we pray."

"Don't worry about anything; instead, pray about everything; tell God your needs and don't forget to thank him for his answers. If you do this you will experience God's peace, which is far more wonderful than the human mind can understand" (Phil. 4:6-7, TLB). "A day hemmed in prayer is less likely to unravel" (Anonymous). God is never more than a prayer away from you. When you feel swept off your feet, get back on your knees. Heaven is ready to receive all those who pray.

"Time spent in communion with God is never lost," says Gorden Lindsay. James Hudson Taylor put it this way: "Do not have your concert and tune your instruments afterwards. Begin the day with God." Martin Luther once said, "I have so much to do today that I shall spend the first three hours in prayer." When you pray, you link yourself with God's inexhaustible motive power.

Too many Christians do not pray; they only beg. Don't just beg. *Talk* to God. Edwin Louis Cole points out, "Wishing will never be a substitute for prayer." Remember that prayers can't be answered until they are prayed. "What things soever ye desire, when ye pray, believe that ye receive them, and ye shall have them" (Mark 11:24).

When we pray, we must also be willing to take the action that God requires for the answer to the prayer. Andrew Murray wrote: "Prayer is not monologue but dialogue; God's voice in response to mine is its most essential part." The prayers a person lives on his feet are no less important than those he says on his knees. "Practical prayer is harder on the soles of your shoes than on the knees of your trousers" (Osten O'Malley).

The highest purpose of faith or prayer is not to change your circumstances but to change you. Pray to do the will of God in every situation; nothing else is worth praying for. Prayer may not change all things for you, but it sure changes you for all things. Prayer is the stop that keeps you going. If God is your Father, please call home.

NUGGET #46

Let Go So You Can Lay Hold.

You're not free until you've been made captive by God's supreme plan for your life. Only those who are bound to Christ are truly free. In His will is our peace.

There is something significant that happens when we become wholly yielded to Him. "For the eyes of the Lord search back and forth across the whole earth, looking for people whose hearts are perfect toward him, so that He can show His great power in helping them" (2 Chr. 16:9, TLB).

"If a man stands with his right foot on a hot stove and his left foot in a freezer, some statisticians would assert that, on the average, he is comfortable" (*Oral Hygiene*). Nothing could be further from the truth. God doesn't want us to live our lives with one foot in heaven and one foot in the world. He wants all of us.

D.L. Moody said: "It does not take long to tell where a man's treasure is. In fifteen minutes of conversation with most men, you can tell whether their treasures are on earth or in heaven." As a young man, Billy Graham prayed, "God, let me do something—anything—for you." Look at the result of that simple but heartfelt prayer.

Those who can see God's hand in everything can leave everything in God's hands. You must let go so you can lay hold. When you have nothing left but God, then for the first time you become aware God is enough. As soon as you decide to not keep anything from God, you show your love for Him. "The most important thought I ever had was that of my individual responsibility to God" (Daniel Webster).

The world has rarely seen what God can do with, for and through a man who is completely yielded to Him. What and how you worship determines what you become. Corre ten Boom advised, "Don't bother to give God instructions. Just report for duty."

Martin Luther sums up being fully yielded this way: "God created the world out of nothing, and as long as we are nothing, He can make something out of us."

NUGGET #47

Don't Postpone Joy.

Enthusiasm makes everything different. You can't control the length of your life, but you can control its width and depth by adding fun and enthusiasm. When you have enthusiasm for life, life has enthusiasm for you. "He that is of a merry heart hath a continual feast." (Prov. 15:15). William Ward said, "Enthusiasm and persistence can make an average person superior; indifference and lethargy can make a superior person average."

"Always be joyful. Always keep on praying. No matter what happens, always be thankful, for this is God's will for you who belong to Christ Jesus" (1 Thess. 5:16-18, TLB). Don't postpone joy. Joy is the most infallible sign of the presence of God. It is the echo of God's life within us. Enthusiasm is an inside job.

If you find yourself dog-tired at night, it may be because you growled all day. Learn to laugh at yourself. A person with a great sense of humor may bore others, but he never has had a dull moment himself. "Of all the things God created, I am often most grateful He created laughter" (Chuck Swindoll). Humor is to life what shock absorbers are to automobiles.

One of the single most powerful things you can do to influence others is to smile at them. You are never fully dressed until you wear a smile. The best facelift is a smile. A smile is an asset; a frown is a liability. Some people grin and bear it; others smile and change it. Shelby Friedman recommended: "Be like the Mona Lisa. She keeps smiling when her back's to the wall."

Both enthusiasm and pessimism are contagious. How much of each do you spread? "It's difficult to remain neutral or indifferent in the presence of a positive thinker" (Denis Waitley).

You can succeed at almost anything for which you have unlimited enthusiasm. "In my experience, the best creative work is never done when one is unhappy," said Albert Einstein. Every success of genius must be the result of enthusiasm. For every opportunity you miss because you're too enthusiastic, you will miss a hundred because you're not enthusiastic enough. I prefer the foolishness of enthusiasm to the indifference of logic.

You will rarely succeed at anything unless you have fun doing it.

NUGGET #48

Build On Victories.

Simply stated, there are two distinct times when a person is most likely to quit; after a mistake or after a victory. How many people of great potential have you known? Where did they all go? Most people of great potential stop because they don't build on their victories.

Success has made failures of many men. So, don't quit after a victory-*build*! If at first you do succeed, try something harder.

Once you're moving you can keep moving. Each victory only buys an admission ticket to a more challenging opportunity. The greatest benefit of a success is the opportunity to do more. "Opportunities multiply as they are seized" (John Wicker). The more you do, the more you can do.

"Perhaps it is a good thing that you haven't seen all your dreams come true. For when you get all you wish for, you will be miserable. To be forever reaching out, to remain unsatisfied is a key to momentum" (*North Carolina Christian Advocate*).

The person who is satisfied with what he has done will never become famous for what he will do. Thomas Edison said, "Show me a thoroughly satisfied man and I will show you a failure."

The first step towards getting somewhere is to decide that you are not going to stay where you are. When you have a victory, comfort and money will come but don't confuse comfort with happiness and money with success. It's not what you get that makes you successful; rather it is what you are continuing to do with what you've got.

Remember this your lifetime through
Tomorrow, there will be more to do
And failure waits for all those who stay
With some success made yesterday
(Anonymous).

NUGGET #49

Love Opens.

"What force is more potent than love?" (Igor Stravinsky). Love is the most important ingredient of success. Without it your life will echo with emptiness. Jesus said, "By this shall all men know that ye are my disciples, if ye have love one to another" (John 13:35). There is a simple way to live a life of love: breathe in God's Spirit, and you'll exhale His love.

Love will find a way. Everything else will find an excuse. "Let love be your greatest aim" (1 Cor. 14:1, TLB).

Love people more than they deserve. Never miss a chance to say a kind word to another person. "You will find as you look back upon your life that the moments when you have really lived are the moments when you have done things in a spirit of love," says Henry Drummond.

"Constant kindness can accomplish much. As the sun makes ice melt, kindness causes misunderstanding, mistrust and hostility to evaporate" (Albert Schweitzer). Kindness has converted more sinners than zeal, eloquence or learning. Practice constant kindness.

Augustine described love: "What does love look like? It has the hands to help others. It has the feet to hasten to the poor and needy. It has the eyes to see misery and want. It has the ears to hear the sighs and sorrow of men." "For a moment, love can transform the world. Love is life...and if you miss love, you miss life" (Leo Buscaglia).

The Bible says, "We know that we have passed from death unto life, because we love" (1 John 3:14). Do all things with love because love opens, love asks, love expands and love creates.

To be loved, be lovable. Make it a point to love someone who doesn't deserve it, and "most important of all, continue to show deep love for each other, for love makes up for many of your faults" (1 Pet. 4:8, TLB).

NUGGET #50

Never Let Yesterday Use Up Too Much Of Today.

Yesterday ended last night. So today it is more valuable to look ahead and prepare than to look back and regret. Don't let regrets replace your dreams. "A man is not old until regrets take the place of dreams" (John Barrymore). Regret looks back. Worry looks around. Faith looks up.

Life can be understood backwards, but it must be lived forwards. If past history was all that mattered, librarians would be the only successful people in the world. The past should only be viewed with gratitude for the good things God has done, so look backwards with gratitude and forward with confidence. Your past is the start of your fresh start.

Consider what Vivian Laramore said, "I've shut the door on yesterday and thrown the key away—tomorrow holds no fears for me, since I've found today." Use the past as a launching pad, not a lawn chair. Dreams of the future are more valuable than the history of the past. "The wise man looks ahead. The fool attempts to fool himself and won't face the facts." (Prov. 14:8, TLB).

Experience is at best yesterday's answer to today's problem. It should only be a guide, not a jailer. Your past is not your potential. Never build your future around your past. The past is over. You must be willing to shed part of your previous life.

God doesn't review your past to determine your future. "Remember ye not the former things, neither consider the things of old. Behold, I will do a new thing; now it shall spring forth; shall ye not know it? I will even make a way in the wilderness, and rivers in the desert (Is. 43:18-19).

"Keep your eye on the road, and use your rear-view mirror only to avoid trouble" (Daniel Meacham). Stop taking journeys into the past. Don't make the mistake of letting yesterday use up too much of today.

NUGGET #51

Alphabet For Momentum.

A. Agreement

B. Boldness

C. Creativity

D. Desire

E. Endurance

F. Focus

G. Gratitude

H. Hope

I. Integrity

J. Jesus

K. Kindness

L. Loyalty

M. Mercy

N. Nurture

O. Opportunity

P. Peace

Q. Questions

R. Risk

S. Servanthood

T. Timing

U. Unity

V. Values

W. Willingness

X. e(X)traordinary

Y. Yearning

Z. Zeal

NUGGET # 52

Everyone Needs A Faith-Lift.

Faith can rewrite your future. "The only thing that stands between a man and what he wants from life is often merely the will to try it and the faith to believe that it is possible" (Richard DeVos). Faith is like a flashlight: no matter how dark it gets, it will help you find your way. "Every tomorrow has two handles; we can take hold by the handle of anxiety or by the handle of faith" (*Southern Baptist Brotherhood Journal*).

Regret looks back; worry looks around; faith looks up. Great leaders have one common spiritual gift—faith. God always holds something for the man who keeps his faith in Him. "...He is a rewarder of them that diligently seek Him" (Heb. 11:6). Your life will shrink or expand in proportion to your faith.

Think like a man of action, and act like a man of faith. Prayer is asking for rain; faith is carrying the umbrella. You must first be a believer if you want to be an achiever. Says Paul Little: "Faith, in its very nature, demands action. Faith is action—never a passive attitude." Faith is not a pill you take but a muscle you use. Faith is when your hands and feet keep on working when your head and others say it can't be done. Active faith is necessary for victory.

By faith you can be decisive in the absence of certainty or in the presence of indecision. It is not daydreaming; it is decision-making. A. W. Tozer wrote: "Real faith is not the stuff dreams are made of; rather it is tough, practical, and altogether realistic. Faith sees the invisible but it does not see the non-existent." Corre ten Boom described faith this way: "It is like radar that pierces through the fog, the reality of things at a distance that the human eye cannot see." The world says seeing is believing. Faith says believing is seeing.

Faith is like a toothbrush. You should have one and use it daily, but you shouldn't try to use someone else's. Ralph Waldo Emerson said, "All I have seen teaches me to trust the Creator for all I have not seen." Doubt is the great modern plague; but faith can cure it. Real faith will refuse to see anything that is contrary to the Bible. It won't look at the circumstances or conditions but at the promise.

Doubt sees the obstacle, faith sees the way;
Doubt sees the darkest night, faith sees the day;
Doubt dreads to take a step, faith soars on high;
Doubt questions, "Who believes?"
Faith answers, "I" (Anonymous).

A FINAL WORD

Be the original person God intended you to be. Don't settle for anything less. Don't look back. Look forward and decide today to take steps toward His plan for your life.

Receive His momentum for your life. Let go of anything that makes you want to stop. Know that God will continue to perform His will in you.

Remember 1 Thessalonians 5:24 when it says, "Faithful is he that calleth you, who also will do it."

Additional copies of
Let Go Of Whatever Makes You Stop
are available at fine bookstores everywhere
or directly from:

Insight International
P.O. Box 54996
Tulsa, Oklahoma 74155
www.freshword.com

Volume discounts available

John Mason welcomes the opportunity to speak to your church, conference, retreat, or to men's, women's, and youth groups.

The following materials by John Mason are available from Insight International :

BOOKS:

An Enemy Called Average

You're Born an Original — Don't Die a Copy

Let Go of Whatever Makes You Stop

Words of Promise

Don't Wait for Your Ship to Come In — Swim Out to Meet It

Momentum Builders

Ask... (Life's Most Important Answers Are Found in Asking the Right Questions)

Conquering an Enemy Called Average

BOOKS-ON-TAPE:

"An Enemy Called Average"

"You're Born an Original — Don't Die a Copy"

"Let Go of Whatever Makes You Stop"

"Conquering an Enemy Called Average"

VIDEOS:

"Momentum: How To Get It, How To Have It, How To Keep It"

"Potential: There is Something Good Inside of You Waiting to Get Out"

ABOUT THE AUTHOR

John Mason is the founder and president of Insight International. The purpose of this organization is to encourage people to use all their gifts and talents while fulfilling God's plan for their lives.

John Mason is in much demand throughout the United States and abroad as a speaker and minister. He is the author of several best-selling books, as well as many tapes and videos.

He holds a Bachelor of Science degree in Business Administration from Oral Roberts University.

John was blessed to be raised in a Christian home in Fort Wayne, Indiana by his parents Chet and Lorene Mason. He, his wife, Linda, and their four children Michelle, Greg, Mike and Dave currently reside in Orlando, Florida.